CAHOKIA
CITY OF THE SUN

Prehistoric Urban Center in the American Bottom

CAHOKIA MOUNDS MUSEUM SOCIETY

COLLINSVILLE, ILLINOIS U.S.A.

Revised 1999

CAHOKIA: CITY OF THE SUN
Published by the Cahokia Mounds Museum Society

Written by Claudia Gellman Mink
Designed by Karen Isam Corley
Edited by William Iseminger

Library of Congress Catalogue Card Number: 92-081951
ISBN: 12345-67890
Printed in the United States of America

Acknowledgements/Credits

Typesetting: Tom Gerwitz Evola
Printing: Color Art
Film separation: Accu-Color
Editorial assistance: Margaret Brown, Doris Marti,
Gloria Iseminger, Albert Meyer, Eric Mink

PHOTOGRAPHY:
Cahokia Mounds Staff: 8 top, 12, 30, 44 top, 46 top left, 47 top left
and right, 58 bottom, 62, 63, 64, 73,75 right, bottom, 76 top left,
bottom; Cahokia Mounds Archives: 35 right, 36; Cahokia Mounds
Museum Society: (Chris Pallozola) 75 bottom; Art Grossman
Photo, St. Louis: 8 top left, 37 bottom; 38, 39, 40, 41, 42, 43, 45
top, 50 top, 71, 72 bottom, 75 top, 76 top right; William Fecht: 22
bottom, 54; St. Louis Science Center: 22 center, 48 left, 52 right;
Donna Lawrence Productions: (Michael Brohm) 13 bottom, 15, 20
bottom, 21 right (2), 22 top, 44 bottom, 46-47 top (corn), 48
bottom, 50 top left, 51, 52 left, 55, 56, 60 top; (Doug McKay) Title
page, 6; Richard Norrish: 50 bottom; Southern Illinois University-
Edwardsville Archaeology Program: 59; University of Wisconsin-
Milwaukee: 60 bottom, 61 top, 65; University of Illinois/Illinois
Department of Transportation: 13 top; Pete Bostrom: 49, 53, 57;
Jane Prince: 76 left center; Stupp Teacher Resource Center,
Missouri Botanical Garden: 46 top right.

ARTWORK:
Albert Meyer: 10 bottom, 34 bottom, 35 left, 49 bottom; Lloyd K.
Townsend: 7, 10-11 top, 16 top, 24-25 top, 29 bottom; Michael
Hampshire: cover, 4-5, 20-21 top; William Iseminger: 23 bottom,
27; Le Page Du Pratz: 16 bottom, 17 top; David Klostermeier: 19
(adapted from Major Stephen Long, 1819); George Bloodsworth:
32; Scott Hull Associates: (Lee Woolery) 44-45 center, 46 left, 53
top, 58 top, (Don Vanderbeek) 48 top right; Paul Bradford: 8-9
center, 31; Karl Bodmer: (Joslyn Art Museum, Omaha, NE) 68
bottom; Faye M. Garvue: (University Microfilms, Ann Arbor, MI)
54-55 bottom; Lopez Needleman Graphic Design: 34 top,
(floorplan) 72.

Contents

INTRODUCTION

A thousand years ago, a civilization more sophisticated and powerful than any other in the Western Hemisphere north of Mexico grew up and flourished in the rich Mississippi River bottom land of southwestern Illinois and environs.

These native American people—who are called *Mississippians* by archaeologists—supported a population as large as 20,000 at their zenith with a wide-scale agricultural economy based primarily on the cultivation of corn. The crops they grew combined with the region's bountiful wildlife and indigenous plants to form a stable, year-round food supply. Such stability and ties to the land gave rise to the formation of permanent settlements that grew into an extensive network of communities with a regional center of metropolitan proportions.

The sedentary lifestyle of the Mississippians made possible other hallmarks of advanced civilization: widespread commerce; stratified social, political, and religious organization; specialized and refined crafts; and monumental architecture, here in the form of earthen mounds covering up to 14 acres and rising as high as 100 feet.

Their extraordinary success continued for five

centuries until, for reasons still unknown, the sun set on the Mississippians as it had on the great Mayan, Egyptian, and Mesopotamian people before them. Finally, when agencies of the state of Illinois carried out the first scientific investigations of the area in the 1920s, the true extent of this vibrant culture began to emerge.

The remnants of the Mississippian's central city—now known as Cahokia for the Indians who lived nearby in the late 1600s—are preserved within the 2200-acre tract that is the Cahokia Mounds State Historic Site. Located just eight miles east of downtown St. Louis, Missouri, near Collinsville, Illinois, Cahokia was designated a World Heritage Site in 1982 by the United Nations Educational, Scientific, and Cultural Organization for its vital contribution to the understanding of North American prehistory.

This book, and the Cahokia Mounds Interpretive Center, attempt to weave as rich a tapestry as possible of life at Cahokia from approximately A.D. 800 to A.D. 1300. Current thinking is based on 70 years of archaeological research and the journals of 16th through 18th century European adventurers who traveled among tribes of what is now the southeastern United States. Scholars believe that much of what the chroniclers noted were Mississippian traditions that survived long after Cahokia's decline. The arrival of Europeans on this continent marks the division between prehistoric and historic times in the study of North American cultures.

The sun to us is the physical representation of the Great Spirit, God: the Power in the Universe.

–Mescalero Apache philosophy

CHAPTER ONE

TIME

SETTING
THE STAGE

B
y A.D. 800, as the Mayans declined in Mexico and Europe muddled through the Dark Ages, Cahokia was ripe for the emergence of a great civilization based on agriculture. The physical and cultural environments there offered the fruits of thousands of years of development to the emerging Mississippian people.

The Physical Setting

In A.D. 800, the climate was similar to that of today. Over the next 400 years, it gradually warmed and was quite moist. Those conditions produced longer growing seasons than in previous centuries.

Cahokia's geographic setting at the confluence of three major rivers and four ecozones was ideal. The meeting of the Mississippi, Missouri, and Illinois Rivers created an exceptionally fertile and expansive flood plain called the American Bottom. It stretched 70 miles along the Mississippi from present day Alton, Illinois, to Chester, Illinois, and was up to 12 miles wide from the river east to its bluffs. In the spring, when rains swelled the bottom land's streams

(PRECEDING PAGE) Paleo-Indian hunters surround a mastodon. The spear, propelled by a device called an atlatl, was the primary weapon of the earliest Native American cultures.

INDIANA

tío River

KENTUCKY

ASTERN
WOODLANDS

ESSEE

ABAMA

(ABOVE) Cahokia's ideal location at the convergence of four ecozones and three major rivers allowed access to many resources from diverse areas.

and their myriad tributaries, water carrying rich silt from the riverbeds renewed the nutrients essential for consistent and wide-scale farming.This extensive network of waterways also gave the Mississippians access to distant areas where they hunted, traded, and learned through contact with other cultures.

The Mississippians found a wealth of natural resources in the ecozones that immediately surrounded Cahokia. The forested Ozark Mountains to the southwest offered important rocks and minerals like granite, sandstone, limestone, and especially chert for making tools. The Ozarks also abounded in white-tailed deer, the Mississippian's primary source of meat and skin for rawhide and clothing. The Prairie to the north and west was a seemingly endless expanse of tall grasses that were useful for building and furnishing homes and other structures. The Woodlands to the east of the American Bottom were rich in nuts and berries, in animal life—white-tailed deer, raccoon, turkey, squirrel, wolf, gray fox, black bear, opossum, and bobcat—and in oaks, hickories, and other deciduous trees that provided excellent hardwoods for canoes, fires, tool handles, bows and arrows, and building construction. The Eastern Woodlands also were dotted with salt licks which yielded essential dietary salt for people and animals alike. And the Mississippi Valley itself gave these farmers not only its rich soil, but also its fish and other aquatic life; ducks, geese, and all the migrating waterfowl that traveled the Mississippi Flyway; game animals including deer, beaver, raccoon, and otter; mulberries, persimmons, nuts, and other edible plants; and a wide variety of trees.

Previous Cultures

The cultural environment of the American Bottom also was right for the appearance of the Mississippian civilization. Advanced technologies and customs these people would incorporate into their own lifestyle already existed, the combined result of several distinct cultures dating back to humanity's arrival in the area at the end of the last Ice Age, about 10,000 B.C.

While the precise origin of the Native Americans eludes us, scientific evidence indicates that their ancestors wandered onto this previously uninhabited continent from northern Asia tens of thousands of years ago. At the time, much of the earth's water was locked up in ice sheets and the lowered sea level exposed a land mass—the Bering Land Bridge—connecting Siberia with Alaska. Discoveries of ancient animal bones in association with prehistoric tools on both sides of the Bering Strait show that Asian hunters followed herds of migrating caribou, mammoths and other animals across the land bridge and into North America, certainly unaware that they

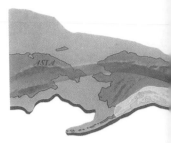

PALEO   ARCHAIC   WOODLAND

Bef 12,000 bCE ~ 8000 BCE ~ 1000 BCE

(ABOVE) Migration route of earliest Americans, descendants of Asian hunters who crossed the Bering Land Bridge from Siberia into Alaska by 12,000 B.C. or earlier. People reached the American Bottom by about 10,000 B.C. *(OPPOSITE)* Diversification of artifact inventory over time.

were going where no one had gone before. A number of now-extinct, Ice Age mammals including camels, horses, long-horned bison, mastodons, giant beavers, dire wolves, and saber-tooth tigers provided them with additional food and materials as did smaller animals and plants.

Over many generations, these Ice Age pioneers and their descendants, known as **Paleo-Indians**, traveled via corridors between the glaciers, slowly spreading throughout North and South America. Spearpoints embedded in the remains of mastodons indicate that they were in the vicinity of the American Bottom twelve thousand years ago. There, as elsewhere, hunting groups of 20 to 30 people lived a nomadic existence, moving constantly with the herds. While our knowledge of Paleo-Indian technology is sketchy, archaeologists believe that the principle weapon both of this culture and the one that followed was the atlatl, or spearthrower, a wooden device used to propel a spear with greater power and speed.

As the earth slowly warmed, the **Archaic** culture evolved by about 8000 B.C. in response to changes in the environment and, as a result, in the food supply. Although the giant mammals of the Ice Age were gradually dying off, smaller game, fish, fowl, and edible plants proliferated in the milder climate. Constant movement in pursuit of sustenance was no longer necessary and because food-getting activities were more localized, people began setting up seasonal camps for hunting and gathering.

The Archaic people were responsible for a number of other significant innovations. They began trading with groups outside the American Bottom; developed spearpoint types that were more efficient for hunting a variety of smaller animals; made axes and seed-processing tools by grinding stone, rather than pressure-flaking or chipping; and started honoring their dead with material items. The Archaic people also carried out the first experiments in cultivation as they observed the habits of wild food plants, gathered the seeds, and attempted to grow them in small gardens. They also built the first mounds.

By about 1000 B.C., the **Woodland** culture had developed throughout most of Eastern North America, appearing in the American Bottom around 600 B.C. Over a period of 1400 years, these people became increasingly tied to the land, more populous, highly organized, and technologically advanced. The considerable time and effort they devoted to honoring and burying their dead indicates that their belief system was relatively well-defined.

As early as 500 B.C., a Woodland subgroup called the Adena built earthen burial mounds in the Upper Ohio River Valley. Following the disappearance of the Adenas, from about A.D. 1 to A.D. 300, the Hopewell subgroup created hundreds of burial mounds and other geometric earthworks in a number of areas in the Eastern Woodlands. After A.D. 500, Late Woodland people living at the convergence of Illinois, Iowa, and Wisconsin produced earthworks called effigy mounds in the shapes of animals. Mound building would become an obsession of people throughout Eastern North America for centuries to come.

The Woodland people also cultivated squash, pumpkins, and other plants, including corn, on a limited basis; built permanent homes; made pottery for cooking and storing food; and established a remarkable trade network. And, at their height, they devised two implements that forever changed the lives of Native Americans: the bow and arrow and the flint hoe.

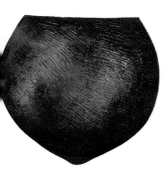

(*OPPOSITE*) *Serpent Mound near Locust Grove, Ohio. A Fort Ancient snake effigy four- to five-feet high, 20-feet wide, and one-quarter-mile long.* (*ABOVE*) *Ceramic cord-marked jar. Late Woodland period.* (*BELOW*) *Copper: raw nugget, pins, celt, bead.*

While there is debate over the genesis of the Mississippians—whether they were immigrants or simply an outgrowth of earlier cultures—there is little doubt that they took inspiration from their Woodland predecessors.

Borrowing from People Elsewhere

Not only did the emerging Mississippians at Cahokia have the benefit of favorable conditions in the American Bottom, but they also profited from contact with other cultures that had developed throughout North America. Interaction with nomadic people on the Plains, forest dwellers in the Northeast, and other Mississippians in the Southeast gave the Cahokians resources and ideas they used to improve upon what they found around them.

From their central location, they traveled vast distances, walking, running, and canoeing along trade routes already established by the Woodland and, to some extent, the Archaic peoples. They got copper from the Upper Great Lakes, mica from the southern Appalachians, and seashells from the Gulf of Mexico. And in the process of obtaining these exotic materials, they observed traditions and lifestyles they would incorporate into their own.

Despite striking similarities to features of cultures in Mexico and elsewhere, there is no scientific evidence that several Mississippian trademarks—flat-topped temple mounds, calendric systems, and ceramic styles—were the result of anything other than independent invention. No Mexican artifacts have been found in the American Bottom or in any other part of this country outside the Southwest.

But above all, the early Mississippians somehow acquired the knowledge of growing corn, or maize, a technology that had originated in Mexico 4000 years earlier and slowly spread to other parts of the Americas. Coupled with improvements in the flint hoe, it was this adaptable and prolific plant, and the steady food supply it created, on which the powerful civilization at Cahokia was built.

Cahokia, North America, and the World in Time

Years	CULTURAL TRADITIONS	CAHOKIA PHASES	ACTIVITIES IN CAHOKIA AREA	ELSEWHERE IN THE WORLD
1800	Historic	Colonial	Trappist Monks	French Revolution
1700			French Chapel on Monks Mound	American Revolution / Horse Introduced to Plains
1600			Cahokia Illini Arrive	
1500	Oneota	Vulcan	Oneota Villages Nearby	Spanish Armada / Columbus Arrives / Inca Empire
1400			Site Abandoned	Aztec Civilization
1300	Mississippian	Sand Prairie	Climate Change / Decline Begins	Marco Polo in Asia
1200		Moorehead	Stockades Built / Peak Occupation	Crusades
1100		Stirling	Woodhenges Built	Toltec Civilization / Vikings in America / Mesa Verde Thriving
1000		Lohmann / Edelhardt	Mound 72 Burials	
900	Emergent Mississippian	Merrell	First Mounds Built	Charlemagne Reigns
800		Loyd	Occupation Expands	Collapse of the Mayans / Effigy Mounds in Iowa
700	Late Woodland	Patrick	First Settlements at Site	Mayan Peak
600				Mohammed Born
500			Villages Nearby and on Bluffs	Black Plague / Fall of Rome
400				Dark Ages Begin
300				
200	Middle Woodland			Hopewell Mounds in Ohio
100			Villages Nearby in Bottoms	Chinese Invent Paper
A.D.				Serpent Mound, Ohio
0 B.C.				Birth of Christ / London Founded
100				
200	Early Woodland			Hannibal Over Alps / China Unified
300			Scattered Hamlets in Area	Punic Wars
400				Olmec Civilization
500				Sparta Flourished / Buddha Born
600				Persian Empire
700	Late Archaic		Hunting Camps	Rome Founded

CHAPTER TWO

CULTURE

THE SCOPE OF ACHIEVEMENTS

For 500 years, Cahokia was the major center of a culture that, at its peak, stretched from Red Wing, Minnesota, to Key Marco, Florida, and across the Southeast. Scholars define culture as the sum of human thought and interaction characteristic of a people or community. Culture includes beliefs, customs, behavior, art, adaptations, and institutions.

Stages of Development

The Mississippian culture evolved in three principle stages at Cahokia as advances in agriculture encouraged population growth and allowed an increasingly settled and prosperous lifestyle.

The Late Woodland Era, A.D. 600 to 800, saw the increasing importance of plant cultivation. Corn arrived in the area and was grown along with squash, gourds, sunflowers, and many seed-bearing plants. As ties to the land grew stronger, settlements became more permanent, technology diversified, and trade spread beyond the American Bottom.

The Emergent Mississippian Era, A.D. 800 to 1000, brought the beginning of much greater

(PRECEDING PAGE) Ceramic bottle depicting mother nursing child. Found in East St. Louis, Illinois. *(LEFT)* Mississippian sites in Eastern North America. Squares: major temple towns with many mounds. Dots: regional centers with several mounds. Triangles: large village sites with a few mounds. The Cahokians traded throughout much of this area, importing copper from the Upper Great Lakes, seashells from the Gulf of Mexico, mica from the southern Appalachians, and other minerals and rocks from the Midwest. *(BELOW)* Deer hunt. From Le Page Du Pratz's The History of Louisiana.

dependence on corn, which became the staple of the Mississippian diet. The population began a rapid increase. Belief systems, community organization, and technology grew more complex. Mound construction started, and the first Woodhenge sun circles were built.

The Mississippian Era, A.D. 1000 to 1400, saw the peak of cultural activity at Cahokia.

The population exploded to as many as 10–20,000 people around A.D. 1050 to 1150. The civilization's remarkable building projects were completed, served their purposes, and were reconstructed as needs and circumstances demanded. Trade and contact with other cultures reached their height.

How We Know

Two sources of information shed light on the story of Cahokia: a few written accounts of early European travelers in the American Southeast, and archaeological investigations that reveal and interpret remains. Archaeologists have confirmed that much of what Spanish, French, and English chroniclers noted, especially among the Natchez in what is now Mississippi, were Mississippian traits that survived centuries after the decline of Cahokia. Taken together, these journals and scientific studies give rise to theories about Mississippian culture in the American Bottom.

In 1539, Spanish treasure hunter Hernando De Soto led the first Europeans on an expedition of the American Southeast, starting out near Tampa Bay, Florida, and eventually coming within 300 miles of the American Bottom. For four years, he and his companions described the Native American lifestyles they observed in Florida, Georgia, the Carolinas, Tennessee, Alabama, and Arkansas, where other Mississippian towns still thrived. Garcilaso De Le Vega reported the accounts of the De Soto expedition in his book, *The Florida of the Inca.*

Twenty years later, English watercolorist John White painted his impressions of the peoples of the south Atlantic coast.

In the 1700s, Frenchmen like Jean-Bernard

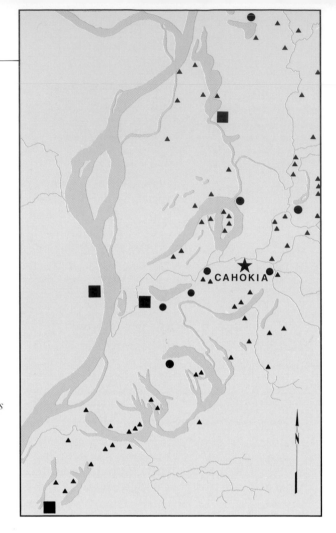

*Mississippian communitie[s] in the American Bottom were situated near the many lakes and streams: **Star**—Cahokia, the first-line community; **Squares**—second-line; **Circles**—third-line; **Triangles**—fourth-line.*

Bossu, Marquette, and Joliet explored and described the Mississippi River and the people who inhabited its valley. The accounts of Le Page Du Pratz, a plantation overseer, are especially rich in details of the rituals and the daily lives of the Natchez and other groups whose culture still was very much Mississippian. His book, *The History of Louisiana*, includes illustrations of both the people and the natural history of the area.

In the late 1800s to early 1900s, anthropologists James Mooney and John R. Swanton recorded their observations of the customs and oral traditions of the peoples of the Southeast. Swanton's research was published in the *Bulletins* of the Smithsonian Institution Bureau of American Ethnology.

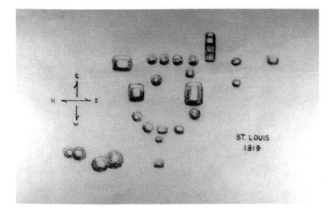

Illustration of St. Louis Mound Group, just north of present-day downtown St. Louis, Missouri (adapted from Major Stephen Long's 1819 map). Once a second-line Mississippian community and suburb of Cahokia. None of the 26 mounds exists today.

Uniquely Organized Communities

In the American Bottom and elsewhere, uniquely organized farming communities were the cradles of Mississippian culture.

Archaeologists recognize four types of Mississippian communities based on their degree of complexity and importance.

The fourth-line community was a small, moundless site that has been characterized as a hamlet, or farmstead, usually consisting of a few structures surrounding a courtyard. These hamlets seemed to have been clustered around larger communities.

The third-line community, a village of several hundred people generally situated on a lake or stream, was made up of homes built around a small plaza and often included one mound. The population of third-line communities probably swelled seasonally when they became processing centers for fish and waterfowl.

The second-line community, or temple town, was a regional center boasting a population possibly in the thousands, an impressive plaza, and several mounds.

The complex, densely populated first-line community was a great capital of politics, religion, commerce, and art with many neighborhoods, plazas, and permanent structures including mounds and temples.

Merchants gather at one of Cahokia's marketplaces, just outside the Stockade walls along Cahokia Creek, to trade wares including shell ornaments, pottery, flint tools, copper, and woven fabrics.

In the entire history of the Mississippian people, Cahokia was the only first-line community. Like great cities today, it had important suburbs, outlying villages, and more remote farmsteads, each tied to the other by a shared lifestyle and each with its vital place in the cultural landscape.

Mississippian Traits

The principal traits of Mississippian culture—flat-topped temple mounds that served as foundations for important buildings and powerful visual reminders of the social order; flood plain agriculture based primarily on the cultivation of corn; craft specialization; extensive trade made possible by an accessible system of waterways and surpluses of grain and materials; and complex community organization determined by kinship, marriage, and alliance—all were inextricably linked in the American Bottom.

There is evidence that Cahokia was a theocratic chieftainship: that is, governed by a leader who claimed divine power. Called the "Great Sun" in later Mississippian cultures, he was thought to be the brother of the Sun and sat at the top of a well-defined social order. Under the chief, his close relatives and other associates formed an elite class. These subchieftains exercised control over heads of family clans who in turn directed the general population.

The enormous scope of its accomplishments attests to the degree of political and social organiza-

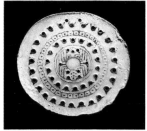

tion at Cahokia: careful urban planning that included areas designated for special use, mobilization of huge work forces for vast numbers of building projects, a complex trade network that traversed a large part of Eastern North America, and well-tended fields capable of feeding a population in the tens of thousands.

The success of agriculture created time for nonsubsistence activities in the American Bottom, a luxury unknown to such an extent in earlier societies north of Mexico. As a result, every aspect of Mississippian culture thrived. Social, political, and religious belief systems grew more elaborate. Specialists—including priests, astronomers, merchants, and a variety of craftspeople—evolved within the work force. Arts, crafts, and technology flourished, growing more diverse and refined.

Music, dance, and sport became integral to daily and ceremonial life.

While temple mounds are the most visible indicators of the Mississippian culture, tangible signs of its richness are evident as well in remnants of other structures and in the countless artifacts that are found throughout the American Bottom.

Huge numbers of Gulf shell beads, for example, and highly decorated objects of shell, mica, and copper tell of leisure time, social stratification, craft specialization, and the surpluses that must have existed to permit the importation of so many costly and exotic goods.

(ABOVE) Carved and engraved shell gorget, Tennessee. Water spider motif (center) may symbolize the sun or "bringer of the sacred fire." Similar gorgets have been found near Cahokia.
(BELOW) Whelk shell beads found at Cahokia. The two dark beads have been charred.

(TOP) Wood duck effigy pot
with rattle in head.
Probably from Cahokia.
(ABOVE) Human head
effigy pot from Arkansas
illustrates forms of facial
tattooing and painting
and ear perforations for
suspension of ornaments.
(BELOW) Cahokia
arrowpoints.

The profusion of Mississippian tool types,
including three kinds of hoes, diverse and specialized ceramic forms, and a wide variety of arrow
points indicates increasing sophistication in production and processing as well as diversification of
activities and food supplies.

Flint clay figurines, incised sandstone tablets,
and effigy pots in human and animal shapes are
clues to perceptions the people of the American
Bottom held both of the natural world and of
themselves. Motifs on such objects are symbols of
life, fertility, strength, and the order of the universe.
The designs also illustrate some of the common
cosmetic techniques the Cahokians employed to
enhance beauty and indicate standing in the
community. They painted the face and body, for
example, with geometric patterns using natural
pigments like ochres and powdered galena and
hematite and tattooed themselves with sharp bone
needles dipped in these pigments. Apparently,
tattooing was common both for men and women.

A True Civilization

By nearly all criteria, ancient Cahokia was a true
civilization—a society marked by social, political,
and cultural complexity and advanced development in the arts and sciences. Cahokia had an
enormous population, diverse art forms, specialized
labor forces, controlled surpluses, long-distance
trade, social stratification, organized government,
monumental public works, and a knowledge of
scientific principles necessary for site planning,
design of a sun calendar, and mound construction.

Nonetheless, one factor prevents a consensus
on this point. Like all Native American cultures
north of Mexico, the Mississippians had no written
language, traditionally a prerequisite for a veritable
civilization. Some form of record keeping probably
existed but we have yet to discover it.

CITY

A PREHISTORIC METROPOLIS

I n A.D. 1150, with a population of some 20,000 people, Cahokia was one of the great urban centers of the world. At the time, it was larger than London and, until 1800, no city in the United States was as sizable as Cahokia at its height.

A massive Stockade enclosed the heart of the city, the political and religious stronghold of the American Bottom. Within its walls were the most important structures and the most elite neighborhoods in the Mississippian world.

Monks Mound
The dominant feature of Cahokia's skyline was Monks Mound, named for French Trappist monks who lived nearby and gardened on the mound in the early 1800s. Situated in the middle of the city, and at the north end of the Central Plaza, this mound covered more than 14 acres and rose in four terraces to a height of 100 feet, making it the largest prehistoric earthen structure in the Western Hemisphere.

Monks Mound is a flat-topped, or truncated,

pyramid, the most common of three Mississippian mound types. Excavations reveal that a massive ceremonial building, probably a temple or palace, stood on the highest terrace and measured 104 feet long, 48 feet wide, and possibly 50 feet high. There, the chief and his priests probably performed religious rituals and administrative duties, surveyed their domain, and greeted emissaries from the hinterlands. Smaller structures and at least two other mounds were built on the lower terraces.

Monks Mound was enlarged several times over a period of 300 years, from A.D. 900 to 1200, then modified slightly until A.D. 1300. Archaeologists calculate that it contains 22 million cubic feet of earth dug with stone tools and carried in baskets on people's backs to the construction site.

Core samples of the mound disclose that Cahokia's engineers used soil of varying textures to build different parts of the mound, assuring proper drainage and structural integrity and indicating knowledge and application of scientific principles.

Large by Any Measure

The neat layout of Cahokia suggests it was a planned city. From atop Monks Mound, one could view many other mounds arranged around plazas. Pathways connected public markets, community-use buildings, exclusive dwellings, distinct neighborhoods, and a sun calendar circle. The homes of most commoners sat outside the walled district.

(PAGE 23) Bird's-eye view of Cahokia at its peak around A.D. 1150. Looking from southwest. (ABOVE) Central Cahokia around A.D. 1100. Viewed from south between peaks of Roundtop Mound, a conical burial mound, and Fox Mound, a platform mound thought to have held a mortuary temple. Paired together opposite Monks Mound, Roundtop and Fox are known as the Twin Mounds. The Grand Plaza and Monks Mound in the distance.

The boundaries of Cahokia formed a diamond shape with Monks Mound at its center. Large, ridge-topped mounds were situated on the diamond's southern and western points and smaller mounds stood along other major axes. The city measured 3 miles east to west and 2.25 miles north to south—in all, 5.1 square miles or 3300 acres. Archaeologists speculate that only 1700 of those acres were high enough to have been inhabitable. Some lower-lying areas, generally considered too damp for residential neighborhoods, were used as quarries for the earth required to build the more than 120 mounds at Cahokia.

If estimates that set Cahokia's population in A.D. 1150 at 10–20,000 are valid, there were up to 4000 people per square mile there. In contemporary America, communities are regarded as cities when there are more than 250 people per square mile.

Unfortunately, Cahokia's dense population eventually experienced what we now call urban stress. Despite unprecedented prosperity, human skeletal remains show that residents suffered from periodic malnutrition and disease. They must have been plagued, as well, with depletion of natural resources, pollution from wood smoke and human waste, and increased competition for space. As these conditions worsened, it is likely that the Cahokians also experienced tightening political control, stricter social distinctions, and increasingly limited access to goods and services.

A Dynamic City

Cahokia was a physically dynamic city, changing throughout its several hundred year history to adapt to cultural and population trends. The Mississippians built over remnants of earlier cultures just as later inhabitants covered Mississippian structures with their own. Urban renewal, it appears, is hardly a modern phenomenon.

Cahokia's two-mile-long Stockade, for example, was built and modified four times over a period of 150 years. But, before the Stockade existed, its route was the site of established residential neigh-

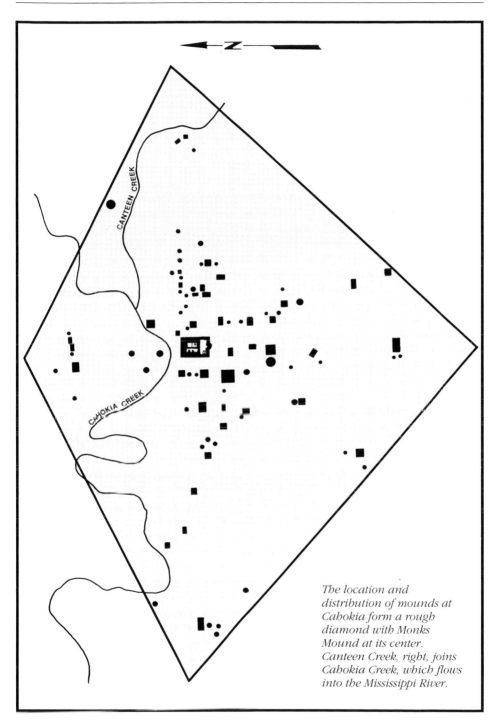

The location and distribution of mounds at Cahokia form a rough diamond with Monks Mound at its center. Canteen Creek, right, joins Cahokia Creek, which flows into the Mississippi River.

borhoods both of Emergent Mississippian pithouses and later Mississippian wall trench houses. As in most excavations of residential sites, refuse and storage pits were found as well. Once the Stockade was built, the area never reverted to residential use.

Between Monks Mound and the Woodhenge, probably outside the Stockade, stood another walled enclosure now referred to as "the compound." This structure, also built over houses, began as a circle and was rebuilt at least two times as a rectangular enclosure with circular projections called bastions. The purpose of the compound is unknown. Eventually, houses were again erected on the site.

The location of the Woodhenge sun circle also was initially residential. During the early Mississippian, the site changed to ceremonial use with the construction of the first Woodhenge, which was enlarged four times over the next 150 years. After Cahokia's decline, the area reverted to a residential function.

Just southeast of Monks Mound was an area that started out as residential, was later abandoned, and became an earth quarry, or "borrow pit." The soil that was removed from this area may have been used to build Monks Mound. Having served its purpose, the depression was filled with trash and soil, capped with clay, and became the site of Mound 51 and its plaza.

One of the more surprising examples of urban renewal at Cahokia surfaced in the late 1980s just outside the Stockade walls in one of the low-lying areas previously thought to have been unsuitable for building homes. Studies carried out on that tract before construction of the Cahokia Mounds Interpretive Center revealed that it was, in fact, once a residential neighborhood and that its houses changed in size, style, and alignment over the years.

Even Monks Mound was built on the site of an earlier village. One wonders if the residents of Cahokia objected to the destruction of their homes for public use, even in the name of the brother of the Sun. The power of eminent domain, apparently, is another fact of life rooted in prehistory.

CHAPTER FOUR

STRUCTURES

MONUMENTS OF A CIVILIZATION

T he Mississippians were accomplished and
prolific builders. They created a wide variety
of structures, from wood pole and thatch
buildings, Stockades, and sun calendars that have
long since disappeared, to the monumental earthen
mounds that endure today. When one considers
how they achieved these feats—felling enormous
logs with simple stone tools and carrying them long
distances without beasts of burden; quarrying
millions of cubic feet of dirt by hand and carrying it
in baskets on their backs—their success is all the
more amazing.

Buildings
The people of the American Bottom developed a
simple and practical method of building construction and adapted it to all their structures whether
large or small, residential, communal, or sacred.

After setting a framework of wooden poles into
a two- to three-foot deep trench, they filled the
trench with dirt and lashed the poles together with
saplings. Both the interior and exterior walls of

some buildings were covered with cattail or reed mats. Others, often the larger buildings, were coated with daub, a stucco-like mixture of clay and grass, applied over a wattle, or lath, of tightly woven saplings. The roofs of Mississippian structures, thatched with prairie grass, were steeply pitched to allow for efficient run-off of rain water.

Excavations for the Cahokia Mounds Interpretive Center revealed over 80 buildings representing four phases of occupation over a 200-year period. Early structures were smaller, rectangular, and had deep floor basins. Through time, the buildings became larger, and eventually were more square with shallower floor basins that almost reached ground level by the final phase.

By far, the most common buildings at Cahokia were single-family dwellings. These probably were windowless and had one doorway covered by a mat or animal skin. While the homes of the elite were larger and sometimes placed on mounds, excavations have shown that most houses were smaller than 20 by 20 feet. Within that space were special areas for making tools, preparing food, storage, and sleeping. The floors of sleeping areas most likely were covered with mats made of bulrushes.

The Cahokians erected a great number of structures for communal purposes. They included: council lodges and open-air summer houses, both used for neighborhood meetings; elevated granaries and other food-storage buildings; sauna-like

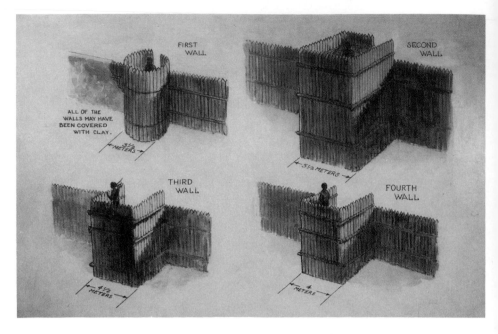

Changes over time in Stockade construction. First wall had round bastions; later reconstructions had square ones. L-shaped entrances for security.

sweatlodges where people, mostly men, went to purify their bodies and spirits; and menstrual huts, where women lived in isolation at the time of menses, when they were feared and shunned.

The largest and most impressive buildings at Cahokia were the temples of religion and government, the grandest being the 5000-square-foot home of the great chief atop Monks Mound. Because these structures were erected on platform mounds, archaeologists believe they were accessible only to high-ranking citizens.

Remains associated with certain structures suggest they were charnel houses, used to prepare the dead for burial. There is evidence that charnel houses sometimes were burned or buried within the mound as part of the funeral ritual.

Stockade

References to walled villages in historic accounts of southeastern Native Americans led archaeologists to look for a fortification at the great capital of Mississippian culture. Aerial photographs taken of fields near Monks Mound in the 1920s and 1930s revealed

light linear streaks that might have been soil disturbances from an ancient wall.

Excavations begun in 1966 eventually confirmed
that an enormous, two-mile-long Stockade surrounded the central portion of Cahokia. The wall
appears to have been started around A.D. 1150 and
then rebuilt three times over a period of 150 years.
Each construction required 15,000—20,000 oak and
hickory logs, one foot in diameter and fifteen feet
tall. The logs were sunk into a trench four to five
feet deep and were likely supported with horizontal
poles or interwoven with saplings. The Stockade
walls may have been covered with clay, as well, to
protect them from fire and moisture.

Because there is no evidence of invasion at
Cahokia, some people question the purpose of the
Stockade. To a degree, it probably served as a social
barrier; however, three things lead most archaeologists to believe that it was primarily a defensive
structure: the great height of the wall; the presence
of evenly spaced bastions, projections from which
archers could shoot arrows; and evidence that
portions of the wall were hurriedly built, cutting
through residential areas, as if danger was imminent.

American Woodhenge

Beginning in 1961, investigations at a proposed
highway site west of Monks Mound unearthed
several huge circles of pits that once contained
enormous red cedar posts. Thought by some to be a
lunar marker or perhaps a sacred enclosure, most
scholars believe it was a solar horizon calendar that
enabled the Cahokians to track the sun's movement
as a way of determining important dates. More
recently, archaeologists have also looked at it as a
posssible alignment device, used to determine the
placement of certain mounds and other landmarks
at Cahokia. The circle was named American
Woodhenge to distinguish it from similar structures
in England.

On the first day of each season, the sun lined
up with specific poles on the circle. And on the all-
important spring and fall equinoxes, which signaled

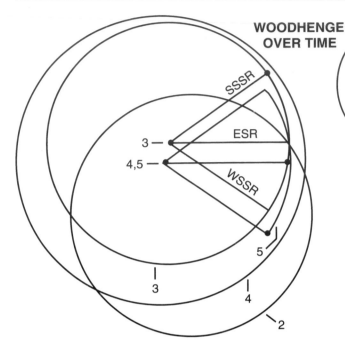

WOODHENGE OVER TIME

The five Woodhenge circles and indentified center points: 1. (240'); 2. (408'); 3. (410'); 4. (476'); 5. (440').

*(**ABOVE LEFT**) Relative size and placement of the five Woodhenge sun circles. SSSR: summer solstice sunrise alignment; WSSR: winter solstice sunrise alignment; ESR: equinox sunrise alignment. (**ABOVE**) Mound 44 superimposes and, therefore, postdates the first Woodhenge, just east of others. (**BELOW**) Drawing of reconstructed ceramic beaker with sun symbols and circle and cross, icons for the world and its four directions. Fragments found at Woodhenge near winter solstice pole.*

the time to begin preparing for planting and harvest, the sun appeared to rise from Monks Mound, home of the chief, believed to have been the brother of the Sun.

Excavations have yielded a total of five circles in roughly the same location, some with a center marker, each slightly larger than the last, and each with an additional 12 poles. The first Woodhenge was made up of 24 poles and the fifth, had it been completed, would have consisted of 72. Why this structure kept changing in size and number of posts remains a mystery.

Soil stains suggest that a fire pit was located near the winter solstice pole at Woodhenge. Perhaps fires burned there to encourage the sun's return from the south. Some of the artifacts found at this spot were decorated with symbols of the sun and may have been used as offerings in the solstice ceremony.

Mounds

The most dramatic monuments of the Mississippian culture are its earthen mounds, more than 120 at Cahokia alone.

(BELOW) The principal Mississippian mound types.
(BOTTOM RIGHT) 1922 aerial photograph of Powell Mound, destroyed for fill dirt 1930-1931. Powell was the third largest mound at Cahokia and the second largest of the city's six ridgetops.

Building mounds consumed vast quantities of time, energy, and soil. The removal of such enormous amounts of dirt created depressions in the earth, now referred to as borrow pits. Once expended, some borrow pits were refilled with the city's refuse, or with soil, to reclaim the land for later use. Others filled with rain and ground water and may have been used as "fish farms" until they became overloaded with silt. Sometimes mounds were built over the sites of filled borrow pits.

Nearly all mounds excavated at Cahokia appear to have been modified over time. Most were built in several phases that included enlargements and additions to the basic structures. Others actually were covered with entirely different mound types.

Mississippian mounds fall into three categories: flat-topped pyramids called temple or platform mounds; conical mounds; and linear ridgetop mounds.

Platform mounds ranging in height from a few feet to 100 feet raised the largest buildings and the people who occupied them above the activities of everyday life. In so doing, they also protected the wood and thatch buildings atop the mounds from

RIDGETOP

CONICAL

PLATFORM

the damp, sometimes flooded, bottomland. Archaeological investigations suggest that these buildings were temples, dwellings of the elite, tribal council lodges, and charnel houses. The majority of mounds at Cahokia were platform mounds.

Platform mounds that may have held charnel houses were sometimes paired with conical burial mounds where the Mississippians entombed people of high status and, sometimes, their relatives and associates. (Most of the population at Cahokia was buried in cemeteries.) Although some conical mounds rose as high as 40 feet, most were considerably lower than platform mounds and ranged in diameter from 20 to 200 feet. Few conical mounds have been explored at Cahokia, and, therefore, our knowledge of them is extremely limited.

The six known ridgetop mounds at Cahokia are especially intriguing to archaeologists because their full purpose is unknown. Four were located at strategic points on the city's diamond-shaped boundaries and its axes and may have been official markers. Excavations of three—Rattlesnake, Powell, and Mound 72—revealed burials.

Cahokia's ridgetop mounds vary greatly in size, from Powell Mound—which before its destruction in 1931 measured 310 feet long, 180 feet wide, and 40 feet high—to Mound 72, 140 feet long, 72 feet wide, and a diminutive six feet high. Despite its small size, excavations of Mound 72 from 1967 to 1971 revealed some of the more astonishing finds in the American Bottom. It actually covered three smaller burial mounds that lay over huge caches of artifacts and the remains of nearly 300 human skeletons, among them mass human sacrifices and the skeleton of what was surely a man of elevated rank, possibly an early leader of Cahokia.

Unfortunately, a combination of natural erosion and modern farming activities has diminished the size and changed the shape of many mounds, in some cases rendering them unrecognizable as man-made structures. Many have been completely lost to the bulldozer and the plow. Fewer than 80 mounds remain today.

Cross-section of Powell Mound showing profile of original platform mound. Sixteen days into its removal, archaeologists were permitted to carry out limited excavations.

CHAPTER FIVE

THE VILLAGE

A CAHOKIAN NEIGHBORHOOD

The family unit was important throughout the American Bottom. Among other things, it served as the basis of neighborhood and community organization.

At Cahokia and elsewhere, members of several generations probably lived in a cluster of single-family dwellings. Within that unit, individuals contributed what was expected of their gender, age, and status to the maintenance of the extended family. These small neighborhoods were fairly self-sufficient, each having its own facilities, like sweatlodges, granaries, and menstrual huts, and artisans who supplied residents with specialized goods and services.

Enclaves of related families, or clans, most likely were grouped together in distinct communities. Each community had special-use buildings—meeting houses, for example—and a sociopolitical structure headed by a male who answered directly to a subchieftain.

During much of the year, neighborhoods bustled with outdoor activity—children playing

games, women grinding corn, and all the comings and goings relating to hunting, fishing, farming, commerce, and construction. In the dead of winter, the neighborhood was quiet, as people lived and worked mostly indoors and prayed they had prepared sufficiently to survive until the time when the sun would return to warm the earth.

The Village in the Cahokia Mounds Interpretive Center uses life-size models to re-create a typical Mississippian neighborhood at Cahokia. The following are scenes from that display.

(PAGE 37) Life-size diorama depicting a typical Mississippian neighborhood at Cahokia. Mirrored walls reflect the scenes, creating the illusion of a large community. Here, an elder storyteller in woven kilt and rabbit skin robe passes a worker stripping bark from logs. Rings of squash, sumac seedheads, and other plants dry on rack; a woman scrapes a deer hide. *(OPPOSITE)* Daily activity in Cahokian neighborhood. The dog was the only domesticated animal at Cahokia. *(ABOVE)* Young woman grinds corn as her mother cooks a meal.

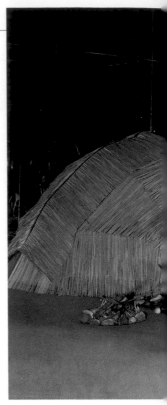

(LEFT) Girl chases boy who has grabbed her doll made of cattail leaves.
(OPPOSITE) Young warrior holding bow watches as potter, surrounded by tools and raw materials of her trade, smoothes interior of ceramic vessel.

Hunter prepares to skin and butcher white-tailed deer while boy heats rocks for the sweatlodge. Steam was considered cleansing for both the body and spirit.

Communal granary where neighborhood residents stored corn, seeds, dried fruits, and meats. Evidence suggests that some early Mississippian granaries may have been elevated for protection against moisture and animals. Nevertheless, a raccoon has invaded the building.

A subchief trades salt for newly completed knife. The flintknapper is surrounded by raw materials of his trade as well as a variety of hoes and knives. The subchief's kilt and sash are woven of plant fibers. The tattoos on his upper arms, face, and shoulders indicate high status.

CHAPTER SIX

LIFE

(PAGE 43) Spring diorama depicts fishing in the American Bottom. The Cahokians used nets, weirs, and bone hooks to catch fish like suckers, catfish, sunfish, and bass. (RIGHT) Characteristic Mississippian artifacts.

MEETING THE CHALLENGES

Despite unprecedented prosperity, life was not easy in the American Bottom. A bad growing season was just the beginning of a long list of potentially devastating challenges the Mississippians faced on an ongoing basis. Meeting those challenges, and all of society's individual and collective needs—economic, physical, spiritual, and emotional—required strict organization, shared beliefs, and leisure activity as well.

A Structured Lifestyle

The four-tiered socio-political hierarchy in the American Bottom gave life a practical structure and direction. The supreme power of the chief emanated from a belief in his divine affiliation and the resulting control he wielded over food surpluses. His priestly advisors were an elite class that directed the community leaders—heads of family clans—to design and supervise agricultural and building projects. The commoners toiled in the fields and in the borrow pits and manufactured the goods needed to support the lifestyle of the ruling class

Beaver effigy pot thought to be from Cahokia. Found in late 1800s.

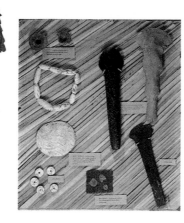

(ABOVE) Cahokia's sociopolitical hierarchy: the chief, subchieftains, heads of family clans, workers. (TOP RIGHT) Ceremonial objects. Clockwise from upper left: copper earspools, ground stone spud, chert mace, copper spud, mica beads, shell beads, shell gorget.

and society at large. Status, gender, age, and kinship all determined each person's precise role in life.

At Cahokia, as in many cultures, men and women had distinctly different roles. Men did strenuous work, made tools, and hunted. They set governmental and religious policy, produced ceremonial art, and taught the older boys. Women, on the other hand, carried out all domestic and child-rearing duties, cultivated crops, gathered plants, processed animal skins and made pottery.

To a great extent, the changing seasons determined the focus of life in the American Bottom. Winter saw an emphasis on indoor tasks, limited hunting in the forests, and, likely, growing anticipation of a time when food would be more plentiful. Spring brought a renewed flurry of activity as life awakened in and around streams and woodlands and as the equinox signalled the time to get ready for planting. In summer, building projects consumed tremendous amounts of time and energy as did cultivation, gathering, hunting, and fishing. The autumn brought earnest preparation for a time when the world would be cold and bleak. Repairs and other building projects were completed. Crops were gathered and stored. Meat and fish were preserved for the hungry months that lay ahead.

Subsistence

Subsistence was a year-round obsession at Cahokia where sustaining the population required massive amounts of corn on a daily basis. While the Mississippians raised several varieties of corn, a diverse assortment of edible plants and animals added limited and seasonal variety to the diet.

The Cahokians grew squash, pumpkins, and sunflowers. They gathered pecans, hickory nuts, and blackberries. They dug tubers such as Jerusalem artichokes and day lilies. They fished and hunted game. And all these food resources were used and processed in a variety of ways. Berries were eaten fresh or dried, for example, and the leaves and shoots used for salads, teas, and seasonings. Sunflower seeds were roasted, mashed into butter, or boiled to extract the oil. Venison was roasted or dried and then left in strips or mixed with nuts and berries. A typical meal at Cahokia most likely consisted of corn served in a variety of forms and a small portion of vegetable stew made primarily of squash, nuts, and pumpkin seasoned with salt, fat, herbs, and, sometimes, bits of meat.

Paradoxically, scholars say that success with corn, the foundation of the Mississippian civilization, had long-term negative effects, both sociological and medical. The enormous population growth that was nurtured by a stable food supply eventually led to the depletion of food and other vital natural resources. And the nutritionally unbalanced diet—

too high in carbohydrates, too low in protein—caused malnourishment and chronic illness. There is evidence, as well, that the Mississippians had a high infant mortality rate, that their teeth wore and decayed prematurely from the bits of stone that were ground into the cornmeal, and that some people actually suffered from starvation during lean winter months.

Leisure Time

Because all work and no play has always made life unpleasant, leisure activities were very much a part of Mississippian culture. At festivals and on ceremonial occasions, the Cahokians enjoyed music, song, and dance and they regularly engaged in games of chance and skill. There was even a "national pastime" at Cahokia that appears to have been every bit as consuming as baseball and soccer are in contemporary cultures. Observations of historic tribes suggest the details of these activities.

The Indians created musical sounds with rattles, drums, and whistle or flute-like instruments. Simple lyrics and chants, probably ritualistic in nature, were sung responsively and accompanied by repetitive, monotone melodies. Dancing was similarly basic and symbolic—a weaving line of people mimicking a snake in a fertility ritual, for instance.

In their free time, the Cahokians played shell guessing games, gambled with dice, and amused themselves by attempting to catch hollow bones on

the tips of pointed sticks to which they were tethered. Like Native Americans of the Southeast and in other parts of the Mississippi Valley, the Cahokians may have played both "hoop and pole" and a stick and ball game similar to lacrosse.

But the premier sport at Cahokia was chunkey, a contest in which two players threw javelins at a rolling, concave stone, attempting to mark the place where it would come to a stop.

Chunkey engaged the entire community, from its youngest members, who apparently played with the miniature chunkey stones that have been found at Mississippian sites, to its leaders, who were buried with the puck-like objects. In fact, later groups in the Southeast took this sport so seriously that they often considered chunkey stones community possessions and contestants called upon the spirits for help by decorating their spears with symbols of swiftness and steadiness. Betting on chunkey was common and, sometimes, as matches continued throughout the day, heavy gamblers lost all their worldly possessions.

(TOP LEFT) Pipe depicting chunkey player, indurated clay. Eastern Oklahoma. (TOP RIGHT) Onlookers cheering contestants in match of chunkey, the premier sport at Cahokia. (ABOVE) Chunkey stone from a cache of 15 in Mound 72.

(ABOVE) *Front of sandstone Cahokia Birdman tablet. Winged warrior with beak of falcon symbolizes both Upper World and This World. Found in 1971 on east side of Monks Mound. (BELOW) Stylized cross-section of Mound 72 showing primary mounds over surface burials and burial pits.*

Beliefs

A shared system of fundamental beliefs was integral to the success of Mississippian culture. Beliefs gave life meaning and purpose and explained the grand scheme of existence.

Like historic Native Americans, the Mississippians recognized a natural order in the universe and attempted to live in harmony with it. Their world was one of opposing forces—dark and light, order and anarchy, good that was rewarded and evil that was punished—and it existed on three levels for them. The light Upper World was steady and predictable. The dark Lower World was unstable and chaotic. In this World, people struggled to balance perfection and utter confusion.

The Mississippians found symbols for those worlds in the animal kingdom. The swift and powerful falcon and eagle represented the Upper World. Frogs, fish, lizards, and snakes were icons of the Lower World. The beaver, owl, cougar, and other animals had characteristics of both. The Mississippians saw symbolism in plants, as well. Red cedar, for example, was revered for its exceptional resistance to disease and decay, for its evergreen quality, and for its deep red color and lasting fragrance. To the Cahokians, all these characteristics were the embodiment of long life.

The Cahokian belief in an afterlife moved them to bury their honored dead with elaborate ritual and with lavish trappings of the life they had led.

The dramatic extent of those rituals came to light with the excavation of Mound 72, a six-foot high ridgetop so small and, at first, seemingly

MOUND 72 CROSS-SECTION

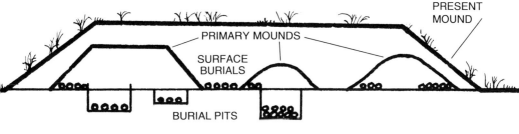

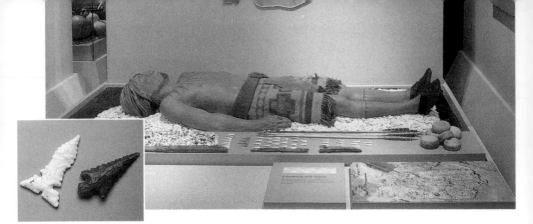

(TOP) Re-creation of burial of early ruler on blanket of 20,000 shell beads. Mound 72. (INSET) Two arrowpoints from burial cache in Mound 72. (ABOVE) Both sides of lower half of Ramey Tablet, engraved with Mississippian war symbols: human heads with beaded forelocks, earspools, hair buns, and pileated woodpeckers. Missing upper half would have mirrored lower section. Sandstone, found in 1800s on Ramey farm east of Monks Mound.

insignificant that it was not even noted on early maps of the area. But three clues led archaeologists to begin digging there in 1967: it lay on the north-south axis of the city; its orientation was diagonal, rather than the usual east to west or north to south; and it belonged to an exclusive club of only six ridgetop mounds at Cahokia.

Their intuition paid off. Over a period of five years, investigations established that Mound 72 actually was built over three small mounds covering surface burials and a series of burial pits. It yielded a spectacular array of grave goods, numbering in the tens of thousands, and also the remains of nearly 300 people. These included young men and women, some of whom appear to have been sacrificed, and the skeleton of an early leader resting on a blanket of 20,000 shell beads. Around him were six attendants and, nearby, caches of mica, rolled sheet copper, 15 chunkey stones, more than 800 perfect flint projectile points, and more beads made of Gulf shells. All this was piled on top of the skeletal remains of three men and three women. In a grave under one of the conical mounds, lay the skeletons of four men without heads or hands, their arms overlapped. Nearby, a deep pit held the remains of 53 young women, arranged in two rows and buried three deep.

Based on radiocarbon dating, scholars believe that Mound 72 and its contents represent ceremonial activity at Cahokia from about A.D. 950 to 1050. The insights they offer about Mississippian beliefs are invaluable, and about one-third of the mound remains unexplored.

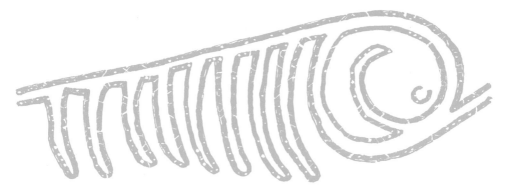

CHAPTER SEVEN

PRODUCTS

USING NATURAL RESOURCES

Imposing monuments and mass human sacrifices excite the imagination and impart valuable information; but, a real sense of a people comes from the myriad products of everyday life.

To make these items, the Cahokians used the plant, animal, and mineral resources available to them in the American Bottom, as well as materials acquired elsewhere through trade. While time and the elements have generally destroyed traces of clothing, baskets, and other items made of fragile, organic resources like animal skin and the inner bark of trees, we know about them through observations of later Indian cultures and decorative designs on pottery and ornaments. Artifacts fashioned from stone, bone, shell, and pottery, on the other hand, have survived the centuries, either whole or in fragments, providing tangible documentation of Mississippian life.

Stone

The Mississippians made nearly all their tools from rocks and minerals, the most durable of natural

(PRECEDING PAGE AND TOP LEFT) Two views of flint clay Birger Figurine depicting woman with hoe cultivating back of cat-faced serpent, a symbol of the earth. The serpent's tail splits into two squash or gourd-bearing vines, which climb up the woman's back. Probably a fertility symbol, this unique artifact was found in 1979 at mortuary site near Cahokia Mounds. (TOP RIGHT) Characteristic Mississippian chert tools. From left: pick, adze, hoe, pick. (TOP OPPOSITE) Flintknapping, the process of making tools from flint, or chert, by striking and pressing off flakes.

resources. Sandstone, granite, and, especially, chert (a form of flint) were abundant and readily available for conversion into a great variety of items through techniques suited to the physical properties of each material.

Sandstone served primarily as an abrasive, like sandpaper or a file, to shape, grind, and polish other objects. It also provided the raw material for figurines, grinding stones, and incised tablets.

The Cahokians used granite, and other especially strong rocks, from the Missouri Ozarks and local glacial deposits to fashion implements that could withstand abuse — axes, chunkey stones, and tools for pounding and grinding seeds, nuts, and grains. Craftsmen pecked these rocks into rough shapes and, when desirable, painstakingly ground and polished them with sandstone.

The vast majority of their tools, however, were made of chert, a mineral common in and around limestone beds of Illinois and Missouri. When struck or pressed at the proper angle, pieces of chert flake off, and the people of the American Bottom exploited this characteristic to create sharp-edged precision implements. The procedure, called flintknapping, required great skill — one wrong strike and a delicate arrowpoint or knife blade was destroyed.

The Cahokians worked chert into a number of tool types including knives, drills, picks, spuds, maces, axes, and projectile points. But it was their

(ABOVE) Back of sandstone Cahokia Birdman tablet. Snakeskin-like crosshatching is symbol of Lower World. Found in 1971 on east side of Monks Mound.

large, specialized hoes—notched, flared, and oval in shape—that can be called the definitive implements of the Mississippian culture. They made soil cultivation far more efficient than earlier periods, allowing corn agriculture, the human population, and culture, in general, to flourish in the American Bottom.

With their well-crafted tools and food surpluses the Mississippians traded for highly-prized mineralogical materials. They obtained raw copper from the Lake Superior area, shaping nuggets into implements and, more often, hammering them into sheets from which they cut effigies and ornaments.

The Cahokians ground galena, ochre, and hematite from southeastern Missouri into paint pigments. They used crystals of quartz from Missouri and fluorite from Illinois, Tennessee, and Kentucky for ornamentation, sometimes pressure-flaking quartz into ceremonial projectile points. They cut beads and other objects of adornment from mica obtained from the southern Appalachians. And they carved Ozark flint clay, fire clay, and other rocks and minerals into animal and human effigies that often showed fashions in hairstyles, clothing, tattooing, and bodypainting. Many of these items were manufactured for ritual use only and were buried with people of high status for use in the next world.

Pottery

While more fragile than stone artifacts, tremendous quantities of pottery in a variety of styles and decorative finishes have survived centuries of burial at Cahokia. These vessels, whether whole or in pieces called sherds, are a great repository of information about Mississippian culture because they were used in nearly every aspect of life.

The Cahokians dug rich clay along stream banks in the American Bottom and in adjacent uplands, carefully removed even the tiniest foreign particles, and then dried it. Next, they added a tempering, or strengthening, agent such as burned, crushed mussel shell (a temper distinctive of the Mississippians), crushed limestone, or crushed

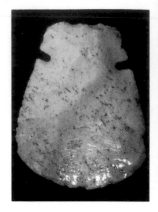

(ABOVE) Mississippian chert hoe. Notches allowed stronger attachment to handle.

LATER

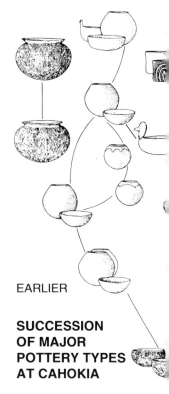

EARLIER

SUCCESSION OF MAJOR POTTERY TYPES AT CAHOKIA

pottery, called grog. They then added water to the mixture, kneaded it, and formed it into a lump.

The Mississippians made their pottery by coiling, or building up a series of rolled "ropes" of clay, and building them up over a shallow bowl-like base to form a basic shape. They blended each successive coil into the previous one using their fingers and a paddle on the outside, a rounded rock or special trowel on the inside. Then they smoothed the vessel with their wet fingers, a mussel shell, or a piece of gourd. They decorated it by incising before firing or engraving fine details afterward; by beating or rolling over still-damp clay with a paddle or stick wrapped in cord; by painting with "slip," a wash of liquid clay mixed with pigment; and by polishing to a high sheen with a smooth stone. After several weeks of drying, the vessel was fired in an open pit.

All the elements of a ceramic vessel are clues to its uses and even to its time and place of origin. The entire progression of pottery at Cahokia can be traced through changes in form and finish.

As with dishware today, vessels of different shapes served different purposes, mostly for food preparation, serving, or storage. There were pans, bowls, plates, beakers, bottles, and jars. Ornaments, engraved beakers and bowls, and effigy bottles, bowls, and figurines in human and animal forms, all may have been used for special occasions.

The Mississippians made large, thick-walled pans for salt production, funnel-like objects with holes in the bottom, and "stumpware," shaped like tree stumps with two root-like legs. Stumpware may have been used to support pots over a fire.

(ABOVE) Ceramic vessels. From left: scallop-rim bowl, long-necked bottle, lug-rim bowl.

Shell

Craftsmen in the American Bottom used both freshwater and marine mollusk shells to make items ranging from common implements to ornaments and burial goods. Because mollusk shells are hard and relatively durable, tens of thousands of shell artifacts have been found at Cahokia, the vast majority of them beads

(TOP) Ornaments made
from shell of whelk.
(ABOVE) Whelk shell from
Gulf of Mexico found in
excavation at Cahokia.

The fast-moving streams of the American Bottom were full of mussels, or freshwater clams. The Cahokians considered the shells of these mollusks more utilitarian than ornamental and used them to make everyday objects like scrapers, spoons, and hoes which they pierced and lashed to wood handles. Burned and crushed mussel shells also served as an effective tempering agent for pottery.

The Cahokians used at least one indigenous freshwater mollusk, the small Anculosa snail, to make beads. They kept the shell intact, but ground it to expose anatomical holes that allowed for stringing.

Through their extensive trade network, the Mississippians imported the shells of saltwater animals like whelks, olivella, and marginella from the Gulf of Mexico. Craftsmen used the broadly-flared outer shell of the whelk to make intricately incised cups and circular gorgets, or pendants. They also used the outer shell to make disk beads by breaking it into small pieces which were smoothed with sandstone and drilled. Tubular beads were made from the whelk's tightly spun inner column by slicing it into long segments and drilling each one length-wise. The smaller, delicate olivella and marginella were left intact but ground like the anculosa to create holes for stringing.

Because these exotic shells were rare and, therefore, expensive, they were owned mostly by people of high station. The discovery in Mound 72 of the ruler laying on a blanket of 20,000 shell beads attests to the prestige they represented in the Mississippian culture.

Wood

For centuries, the dense forests in and around the American Bottom were sources of tremendous quantities of wood essential to the Cahokians' existence. In addition to providing the raw materials for four Stockades, five Woodhenges, and thousands of buildings, trees were used in the manufacture of tools, weapons, handles, baskets, bowls, oils, dyes, foodstuffs, and canoes. And without wood fuel, warm winters, cooked food, and fired pottery would have been impossible.

Probably the most challenging of the Cahokians' wood products were their dugout canoes, made from thick logs of oak, poplar, tulip, and cottonwood. Canoe makers hollowed these logs, which weighed up to 2000 pounds, by alternately burning, scraping, and chopping the desired area. Finished canoes varied in size from 12 feet to 70 feet long.

Making bows and arrows also kept craftsmen extremely busy. Osage orange and hickory both provided the right combination of toughness and flexibility for bows, which were strung with sinew or rawhide. Straight willow, native cane, and maple shoots worked best for arrow shafts, which were tipped with points made of antler, wood, or stone and then feathered to assure straight flight.

Some scholars suggest that thousands of campfires burned day and night at Cahokia's height. If that estimate is even close, fires must have created a tremendous smog problem and, in combination with the hundreds of thousands of trees used for building projects, eventually depleted the forests for miles around.

Animal

The Mississippians made full use of the animals they hunted, whether fish or fowl, mammal, reptile, or amphibian. They made needles of catfish spines, for example, and sequin-like baubles from gar scales. Turtle shells became bowls, rattles, combs, and ornaments; animal fat a soothing ointment. The talons, bones, and feathers of falcons, hawks, and turkeys were fashioned into tools, necklaces, capes, headdresses, and other decorative items. Snake rattles and bear claws made powerful symbolic ornaments. And the skins of opossum, bears, rabbits, and raccoons were made into bags, blankets, robes, and other items of clothing.

By far the most important animal resource in and around the American Bottom was the white-tailed deer, valued not only for its flesh and organ meat, but also for its antlers, hooves, and everything in between. The Cahokians used antlers for arrowpoints, ceremonial headdresses,

Bone and antler tools. Clockwise from left: antler harpoon point, bone awls, bone fishhooks, bone arrowpoints. Center: antler arrowpoint.

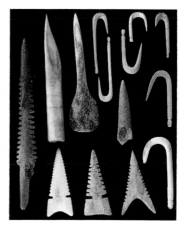

(*ABOVE*) *A Cahokian chief in ceremonial garb. Headdress made of hawk, owl, eagle, or woodpecker feathers; earspools of wood, copper, stone, or shell; cape of beads and feathers; flint mace in hand; woven kilt with geometric designs; deerskin moccasins; shell bead ankle, calf, and wrist bracelets; shell pendant. (*BELOW*) Fingerweaving a sash in the Mississippian tradition. Looms probably were not used in the American Bottom.*

flintknapping tools, and pins for garments and the hair. They made scrapers, hammers, ornaments, fishhooks, needles, awls, and weaving tools from bones. Hooves became medicine, glue, and rattles and sinew served as bindings.

The Cahokians even used the brains to process skins for clothing. Rawhide—the result of stretching, scraping clean, and drying a skin—made strong bindings, but was too stiff to be worn. In order to make garments, the Cahokians simmered rawhide in a brain soup and then massaged more of the greasy organ into the hide to further soften and protect it. They stretched and dried this "tanned" hide and rubbed it with smooth stones, finally smoking it over a slow fire to assure that it would remain supple even after getting wet.

Fiber

The people of the American Bottom exploited plant and animal resources to produce a variety of fiber items. They used the stalks and leaves of tall prairie grasses as thatch for houses, temples, and other buildings. They made fine baskets and fabrics from the inner bark of the cedar tree; woven floor mats from the flexible stems of bulrushes; and sewn mats that covered walls, roofs, and doorways from cattail leaves. The Cahokians spun animal fur and silky fibers from plants like milkweed and dogbane into thread which they used to fingerweave sashes and produce other fabrics. The inner bark of basswood, ash, cedar, willow, and hickory were twisted into cordage. Braided strips of rawhide made especially strong cord and bowstrings, and, because of the tendency of rawhide to shrink as it dries, it created a tight attachment between tools and handles.

While these materials were fragile and decomposed quickly, ancient fires actually burned bits of them into charcoal. As a result of analyzing carbonized fibers, archaeologists have identified the original materials and formulated ideas about techniques the Cahokians most likely employed to process them.

KNOWING

KNOWLEDGE FROM THE EARTH

A lthough only 1 percent of Cahokia has been scientifically explored, most of the site is now protected by state and federal law. Scholars therefore have the luxury of proceeding more deliberately than in days past when the constant threat of land development required salvage excavations to collect as much data as quickly as possible before it was destroyed by construction. What remains to be examined is a vast and priceless reservoir of information about prehistoric lifeways, Mississippian and others, in the American Bottom.

Buried within the earth, each artifact, each soil discoloration, each piece of organic material reveals insights into life at Cahokia. A single fragment of a pot's rim, for example, yields information about ceramic styles, composition, settlement dates, and interaction with other cultures. A cache of unusually fine projectile points near a burial sheds light on natural resources, social structure, the status of the deceased, belief in an afterlife, and tool-making techniques. Human skeletal remains reveal facts

about diet, disease, life expectancy, and burial customs. And stains in the soil (archaeologists call them "features") indicate building projects, cooking pits, and refuse pits that contain a wealth of data in the form of society's cast-offs.

The Science of Archaeology

Archaeologists are scientists who gather evidence in the field, in the lab, and in the library, where they study valuable historical accounts, settlement records, written scientific reports, and raw data. They then analyze and interpret that data in order to formulate, support, or disprove theories about human physical and cultural development.

Field work, commonly called a dig, follows an established procedure of painstaking excavation and meticulous documentation of every find, no matter how small. Whether fragments of possible or confirmed artifacts, bits of carbonized fiber or seeds, or areas of discolored soil, everything is potentially significant. Because the context of a discovery is critical to its full interpretation, detailed descriptions, maps, photographs, and notations of all nearby artifacts, organic remains, and features are essential.

Once unearthed and recorded, materials move on to a laboratory where they are carefully cleaned, labeled, and processed for analysis, interpretation, and storage. Methods of analyzing archaeological evidence range from simply looking at an item and comparing it with already-identified materials, to

using highly sophisticated technology that allows study on an atomic level. This information eventually finds its way into libraries, where it can be used for further research and interpretation.

Interpretation takes the results of analysis and research and gives them meaning. It combines the who, what, where, when, and why of a find and uses that data to shape new theories and test existing ones. Take, for example, an arrowpoint found at Cahokia. Scholars may determine that it is made of chert from Arkansas while its style indicates it was manufactured in Oklahoma. One interpretation of this discovery is that the Cahokians engaged in long-distance trade.

Gathering Evidence

The decision to excavate a particular site may be based on clearly visible features, a mound for example. But more often, sites are less obvious and show up when plows overturn debris or when aerial photographs indicate unusual soil disturbances that appear to be the result of human activity. Legends, infrared photographs, old documents, previous or chance discoveries, electrical and magnetic detectors, even radar, and, certainly, instinct all may lead archaeologists to a good site.

(ABOVE) Archaeological techniques including shovel scraping, screening, and mapping at east portion of Stockade. (TOP OPPOSITE) Field worker using specialized tools and brushes to excavate material in refuse pit. (OPPOSITE) Mapping the patterns of archaeological features.

The first step in a scientific investigation is surveying the site and collecting any artifacts that may lay on the surface, noting their distribution and concentration.

Next, archaeologists divide the area into a working grid made up of squares two meters on a side. Digging begins with the removal of the uppermost eight to twelve inches of soil, called the plowzone. Because this layer is likely to have been adulterated by farming or other modern activities, it is not treated as meticulously as the rest of the site. As shovels or heavy equipment bring up artifacts and other materials, they are mapped, collected, and sent to a lab.

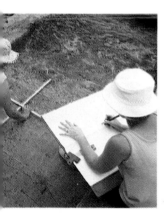

With the plowzone gone, archaeologists dig down in levels. The depth of each level is either arbitrarily determined (usually about ten centimeters) or decided by some natural or artificial clue in the earth. With the utmost care, field workers use shovels, trowels, and brushes to expose and clean their finds. Even rocks that appear to be foreign to the site may be valuable.

Soil discolorations frequently indicate postholes, wall trenches, hearths, refuse pits, and storage pits. Once exposed to the dry air, these features fade, so it is vital that they be mapped, described, and photographed as quickly as possible.

Because soil often contains minute fragments of archaeological evidence, the two must be separated. This is accomplished either by screening—manually pushing fine dirt particles through a horizontal wire mesh tray while trapping larger materials on top— or by floatation, a procedure in which soil is mixed with water and chemicals. Lighter particles like seeds and charcoal float to the top of the mixture. Larger, heavier materials settle on the screen at the bottom of the container.

Analyzing Discoveries

Raw archaeological material is analyzed in laboratories where scientists look for answers to questions of age, composition, use, source, and method of manufacture, among others.

"How old is it?" is of primary importance to the archaeologist. The age of a find puts it in context and helps date material discovered nearby. Generally, the oldest layers, or strata, in which evidence is found are at the bottom, the most recent on top. This principle helps determine the relative ages of materials found in different strata.

More specific dating techniques can be as simple as recognizing a tool style unique to a particular period or as sophisticated and absolute as analyzing atomic particles. Certain techniques apply only to certain materials.

Thermoluminescence and archaeomagnetic dating, for example, yield the age of clay that has been heated to extremely high temperatures. Thermoluminescence also reveals the source of the material and the temperature at which it was fired. Radiocarbon dating determines the age of plant and animal remains by measuring the amount of residual Carbon 14, a radioactive isotope of carbon present in all living things that decays at a predictable rate after death. In some areas, where climate

favored preservation of a whole or partial log, dendrochronology, or tree-ring dating, can be used to tell the age of wood remnants.

Other analytical techniques look at amino acids, uranium levels, quantities of water in pressure-flaked obsidian, and other variables to yield a diverse array of information. Microscopic analysis shows cell structure, allowing identification of species of animal and plant remains as small as a single grain of pollen. The examination of human bone tells of nutrition and disease. Seed identification gives clues to agricultural and dietary practices and climatic conditions. Analysis of stone tools indicates function, origin of material, and method of manufacture.

Interpreting Data

As analysis produces data, scholars look for patterns and interpret them through inductive or deductive reasoning.

Inductive reasoning examines information and proceeds from specifics to a generalization.

For example, if fragments of shell-tempered pottery and carbonized corn were found together, one conclusion archaeologists might draw is that the site was Mississippian.

Deductive reasoning starts with a generality and uses it to make predictions. For instance, archaeologists digging atop a large platform mound might expect to find the two to three feet deep wall trenches of a sizeable building.

Scholars also can combine everything gleaned from research and site analysis to formulate and test new explanations. The synthesis of library research on climate, discoveries in the field about population, and laboratory data on pollen suggest a trend that links climatic change to Cahokia's decline, for example.

Eventually, archaeologists report, or publish, their findings, allowing other scientists to use their data or challenge them in the future. Today, as in all fields, computers are invaluable in managing archaeological data.

CONCLUSION

After decades of archaeological exploration, the sun has just begun to rise on the great Mississippian civilization of the American Bottom. Today, Cahokia and its suburbs hold many mysteries, and they will be the subject of scientific investigations for years to come.

Among the most significant questions is the decline and eventual abandonment of Cahokia beginning about A.D. 1250. Excavations have yet to yield signs of epidemic, invasion, or natural disaster so catastrophic that it would account for the demise of an entire society. Why, then, did this people of unparalleled wealth and power cease to exist?

Today, most scholars point to the convergence of a number of factors, primary among them climatic change and unrelenting exploitation of the land and forests. Cutting trees eliminated habitats for animals and plants used for food and other resources. Denuded bluffs eroded, filling bottomland streams with silt and increasing localized flooding.

Evidence indicates that shifts in weather patterns in the mid-section of the continent starting around A.D. 1250 brought on cooler, drier summers and shorter growing seasons. That deviation would have affected the production of corn, Cahokia's primary food source, as well as the existence of other flora and fauna.

Analyses of human skeletal remains show that, even at the height of Cahokia's agricultural productivity, its people were malnourished by the excessively high carbohydrate diet and seasonal scarcity of food. Such poor nutrition caused serious medical problems including iron deficiency anemia; arrested growth of the longbones; a high infant and juvenile mortality rate; and dental disease, twice as prevalent in the Mississippian as in the preceding Woodland period. Other ailments—arthritis, endemic syphilis, and tuberculosis caused by a fungus borne in soil—all were common at Cahokia. Increasing exposure to new diseases through contact with people outside the American Bottom, cramped living space, and pollution from smoke and human waste must have exacerbated medical conditions. At best, the average life expectancy was only 35 to 40 years.

Surely, this upheaval had other serious social repercussions as well as religious and political ones. Cahokia's leadership, in a futile attempt to maintain control over a severely troubled society, probably tightened its grip on all facets of life including access to basic resources, materials, facilities, and even to the spiritual world. The disillusioned and dwindling masses might have rebelled against such repressive and ineffective government officials and priests, perhaps believing they had lost favor with the gods. Eventually, the Cahokians began to develop new ways of coping with life's stresses, embraced other cultures, and dispersed to more viable environments.

The American Bottom saw one last prehistoric culture before the Europeans arrived. The Oneota people, distinguished from the Mississippians by their distinctive pottery and a unique scraping tool, lived there in small, scattered villages. They hunted, gathered, and farmed on a limited basis and may have built some earthworks.

The origin of the Oneota is unknown; however, archaeologists consider them direct ancestors of the Iowa, Winnebago, Oto, Kansa, and the Missouri, all historic Native American tribes of the Central and Upper Mississippi Valley. Not only did these later groups inhabit the same territory as the Oneota, but they also utilized similar artifacts and symbolism.

In the mid-to-late 1600s, several subtribes of the Illini lived in the vicinity of the American Bottom, notably the Kaskaskia, Tamaroa, and Cahokia. It was they who the early French explorers encountered and whose names have been given to local streams, towns, and even to the mounds.

CAHOKIA AFTER THE MISSISSIPPIANS:

AD. 1400-1600
Cahokia abandoned, Oneota culture settlements in region.
Mid-1600s Illlini Indians move into area, including Kaskaskia, Tamaroa, and Cahokia subtribes, living near Mississippi River.
1673 Marquette and Joliet first Europeans to pass through on Mississippi.
Late 1600s French missionaries and settlers arrive in region.

1700s

1730 French priests build a chapel on first terrace of Monks Mound after relocating Cahokia Indians nearby.
1760s Spanish and British move into area.
1796 General George Collett reports on mounds, and includes Pulcher site mounds on a map.

1800s

1809 Nicholas Jarrot acquires land including the mounds.
1809–1813 French Trappist Monks settle on Cahokia site, on a mound, and plant gardens on the biggest mound, later named for them.
1811 Henry Brackenridge visits the site and the Monks, and reports in a St. Louis newspaper, and later some books. First widely published information on Cahokia site.
1819 Major Stephen Long maps the St. Louis mound group.
1831 Amos Hill builds house on top of Monks Mound.
1833 Karl Bodmer, famous artist, sketches Monks Mound and the Twin Mounds.
1841 J.C. Wild visits site, collects artifacts, and sketches mounds.
1860s Dr. Charles Rau of Smithsonian establishes evidence of occupation from Cahokia to the Mississippi along Cahokia Creek.

• Ramey family purchases center of site and builds new farm complex.
1870s–1880s J.J.R. Patrick surveys and produces first detailed map of site, as well as East St. Louis and St. Louis mound groups. Conducts surface collections and some digging at site. Publishes on site with F. W. Putnam.
1880s–1890s William McAdams and son Clark survey site for Smithsonian, make collections, publish reports, and prepare exhibit on Illinois archaeology and Cahokia for the Columbian Exposition in Chicago.
• Stephen Peet publishes report on Cahokia and area mounds, and engraved stone tablet from the site.

1900s

1904 David Bushnell surveys American Bottom and publishes on important sites.
1920s Warren K. Moorehead conducts first professional archaeological excavations at site, testing several mounds and villages.
1922 Bushnell publishes a report on second line communities in the area and the first aerial photographs of the Cahokia site by Lts. Goddard and Ramey.
1925 State of Illinois acquires 144 acres, creating Cahokia Mounds State Park.
1930 Combination ranger's residence/museum opens on site.
1930-31 Paul Titterington, A.R. Kelly, William McKern, and Thorne Deuel record the destruction of the Powell Mound and do limited testing. Gene Stirling investigates a small mound south of Powell Mound.
1938 Paul Titterington publishes *The Cahokia Mound Group and*

Its Village Site Materials, which includes a record of the Powell Mound investigations.

MODERN ERA OF INVESTIGATIONS AND DEVELOPMENTS

1941 Illinois State Museum conducts salvage excavations on Mound 55 in new subdivision being built south of Monks Mound.
1950s Washington University tests several mounds from Powell Tract west to East St. Louis, and the large Kunnemann Mound at the north edge of the site.
• University of Michigan surveys the American Bottom and conducts excavations in Mound 34 and near Mound 42.
• The Gilcrease Institute excavates in Mound 34 and the field northeast of Monks Mound.
• The Illinois State Museum tests Mound 31 before the destruction of it and Mound 33 for Grandpa's store.
1960s Excavations by the Illinois Archaeological Survey, the Illinois State Museum and University of Illinois, salvage areas to be impacted by construction of Interstate 55/70 through the site. Includes the discovery of Woodhenge on Tract 15-A, the Compound on Tract 15-B, work in the Powell Mound area and other areas in the highway right-of-way.
• Washington University conducts excavations on top of Monks Mound and takes solid-core drill samples through the mound, examining its interior.
Late 1960s early 1970s The University of Wisconsin-Milwaukee conducts large-scale mapping project for Cahokia site and excavations in Mound 72, on the First Terrace and East Lobes of Monks Mound, on the East and South

HISTORY AND RESEARCH

Stockades, on a possible causeway, and in other areas. They also do a controlled surface collection in the Ramey Field.

• The University of Illinois excavates on the First Terrace of Monks Mound, revealing information about mound construction techniques, in the sub-Mound 51 borrow/refuse pit, and on the Powell Tract.

• Washington University excavates on the Fourth Terrace and the South Ramp of Monks Mound, identifying the large building on top and the location of a stairway on the ramp.

• Beloit College works in the Merrell Tract looking unsuccessfully for the West Stockade, but finds much habitation information.

1970s The University of Wisconsin-Milwaukee, The Illinois State Museum, and the Cahokia Mounds Museum Society continue excavations of the East Stockade.

• The University of Illinois-Chicago Circle tests in the large borrow pit, assists with Stockade excavations, and excavates more of the Woodhenge complex. In conjunction with the University of Wisconsin-Milwaukee, they test an area on the Dunham Tract for a possible new museum construction site.

• The University of Illinois continues field school projects at the Powell Tract.

• Old Museum expanded and experimental houses constructed.

1980s Land acquisition increases as homes in the Ramey subdivision are being purchased for removal for the planned new museum; the Rattlesnake Mound tract and the Kunnemann tract added to the site.

• The University of Wisconsin-Mil-

waukee and Southern Illinois University at Carbondale conduct tests in a new tract proposed for construction of a new Interpretive Center, referred to as ICT-I, finding little Mississippian habitation, but a buried Late Archaic horizon.

• The Cahokia Mounds Museum Society Field School conducts excavations on the East Stockade, Woodhenge, and Mound 50.

• Southern Illinois University at Edwardsville conducts testing and full-scale excavations at Interpretive Center Tract-II (ICT-II) for the construction of the new Center, finding valuable settlement information and three previously unidentified mounds.

• New slumping on Monks Mound results in examination of slump areas by Illinois State Museum and Southern Illinois University at Edwardsville, and a new set of core samples is taken from the mound.

1984 Governor Thompson releases funds for the construction of the new Interpretive Center.

1985 The Woodhenge is reconstructed at the original location.

1988-91 Southern Illinois University-Edwardsville conducts field schools, remote sensing projects, excavations, and other research at the site, on the South Stockade, in the Plaza, borrow pits, the Kunnemann Tract, Monks Mound, and other areas. University of Wisconsin-Milwaukee explores the Mound 72 area for another possible Woodhenge structure.

1989 The new Interpretive Center opens September 23.

1990s SIUE conducts test excavations on Mound 56, the Tippets Mound Group, the Little Twin Mounds, the Rouch Mound Tract, promontory mounds, Mound 48,

and continued remote sensing at these and other locations.

• University of Oklahoma field school tests Mound 49, identifying at least two construction stages and other features.

• State University of New York-Buffalo monitors and tests trenches for new water lines going through the Grand Plaza and picnic grounds. Project confirms that Plaza was built up and leveled.

• Researchers reexamine materials recovered in the 1960s from borrow pit below Mound 51, and from 1950s digs in Mound 31.

• University of Wisconsin-Milwaukee continues exploration for a Woodhenge near Mound 72 and trenches nearby Mound 96.

• Northwestern University and Western Michigan University field schools begin multi-year project to locate stockade around western and northern portions of the site.

• SIUE tests Monks Mound prior to installation of new permanent stairways, locating historic and prehistoric features. An unidentified stone mass is encountered 40 feet beneath the second terrace when slump repairs and horizontal drains are installed.

• Central Mississippi Valley Archaeological Research Institute (CMVARI), Washington University, and Northwestern University reopen 1950s excavation in Mound 34 to reexamine soil profiles and features.

• Washington University and Northwestern University conduct tests at the Fingerhut Tract at the western limits of the Cahokia site.

• *Ancient Skies and Sky Watchers of Cahokia* and *Platforms of Power* archaeological conferences held at the site.

Recommended Reading

To learn more about the prehistory of the American Bottom,
the Mississippian culture, and Cahokia:

* Bareis, Charles J. and James W. Porter, editors. *American Bottom Archaeology.* Urbana: University of Illinois Press, 1984.

* Brown, James A., editor. *Perspectives in Cahokia Archaeology.* Urbana: Illinois Archaeological Survey, Bulletin No. 10, 1975.

Emerson, Thomas E. *Cahokia and the Archaeology of Power.* Tuscaloosa: University of Alabama Press, 1997.

* Emerson, Thomas E. and R. Barry Lewis, editors. *Cahokia and the Hinterlands: Middle Mississippian Cultures of the Midwest.* Urbana: University of Illinois Press, 1991.

* Fowler, Melvin L., editor. *Explorations into Cahokia Archaeology.* Urbana: Illinois Archaeological Survey, Bulletin No. 7, second edition, 1977.

* Fowler, M 'vin L., editor. *The Ancient Skies and Skywatchers of Cahokia: Woodhenge, Eclipses, and Cahokian Cosmology.* The Wisconsin Archaeologist, Vol. 77, No. 3/4. Madison, 1996.

Fowler, Melvin L., *The Cahokia Atlas: A Historical Atlas of Cahokia Archaeology.* Revised edition. University of Illinois at Urbana-Champaign, Studies in Archaeology No. 2, 1997.

Fowler, Melvin L. and Robert L. Hall. "Late Prehistory of the Illinois Area." In *Handbook of North American Indians.* Bruce G. Trigger, editor. Vol. 15. Washington D.C.: Smithsonian Institution, 1978.

Iseminger, William. "Mighty Cahokia." *Archaeology Magazine.* Vol. 49, No. 3. New York, 1996.

Kennedy, Roger G. *Hidden Cities: The Discovery and Loss of Ancient North American Civilization.* New York: The Free Press, 1994.

Mehrer, Mark W. *Cahokia's Countryside: Household Archaeology, Settlement Patterns, and Social Power.* DeKalb: Northern Illinois University Press, 1995.

Milner, George R. *The Cahokia Chiefdom.* Smithsonian Press, 1998.

Milner, George R. "The Late Prehistoric Cahokia Cultural System of the Mississippi River Valley: Foundations, Florescence, and Fragmentation." *Journal of World Prehistory,* Vol. 4, No. 1, 1990.

Pauketat, Timothy R. *The Archaeology of Downtown Cahokia.* Urbana: Illinois Transportation Archaeological Research Program, 1999.

Pauketat, Timothy R. *Temples for Cahokia Lords.* Museum of Anthropology, University of Michigan, Memoirs No. 26. Ann Arbor, 1993.

Pauketat, Timothy R. *The Ascent of Chiefs: Cahokia and Mississippian Politics in Native North America.* Tuscaloosa: University of Alabama Press, 1994.

* Pauketat, Timothy R. and Thomas E. Emerson, editors. Cahokia: *Domination and Ideology in the Mississippian World.* Lincoln: University of Nebraska Press, 1997.

Skele, Mikels. *The Great Knob: Interpretations of Monks Mound.* Studies in Archaeology No. 4. Springfield: Illinois Historic Preservation Agency, 1988.

* Smith, Bruce D., editor. *Mississippian Settlement Patterns.* New York: Academic Press, 1978.

* Stoltman, James B. editor. *New Perspectives on Cahokia: Views from the Periphery.* Monographs in World Archaeology No. 2. Madison: Prehistory Press, 1991.

Time Life Books, editors. *Mound Builders and Cliff Dwellers.* Lost Civilizations Series, 1992. *The First Americans.* American Indian Series, 1992.

* These edited volumes contain articles by numerous archaeologists on Cahokia-specific and Cahokia-related topics.

ABOUT CAHOKIA TODAY

The Cahokia Mounds State Historic Site today encompasses some 68 of the original 120 mounds, including Monks Mound, and a comprehensive, state-of-the-art interpretive center that brings the Mississippian civilization to life for hundreds of thousands of visitors each year.

The Interpretive Center

The Cahokia Mounds Interpretive Center uses a full range of contemporary museum display techniques to weave the tapestry of local prehistoric life. Subtle sound effects and Native American music enhance the visual exhibits.

In the lobby, a large-scale model shows the principal known features of ancient Cahokia and observation windows offer a panoramic view of the immense Monks Mound just across the site of the Grand Plaza.

Visitors emerge from the orientation theater and its award-winning multimedia show into a spectacular mirrored re-creation of a Cahokian neighborhood in A.D. 1150. Life-size models cast from living Native Americans depict typical activities of daily life from grinding corn and making projectile points to

(*ABOVE*) *Lobby of Cahokia Mounds Interpretive Center. Foreground: model of Cahokia Mounds. Background: glass wall allowing view of Grand Plaza and Monks Mound.*

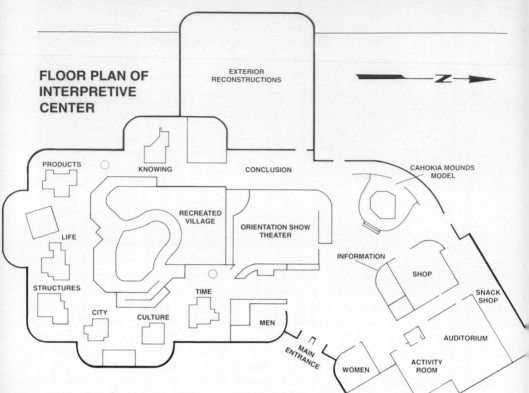

FLOOR PLAN OF INTERPRETIVE CENTER

EXTERIOR RECONSTRUCTIONS

PRODUCTS

KNOWING

CONCLUSION

CAHOKIA MOUNDS MODEL

RECREATED VILLAGE

ORIENTATION SHOW THEATER

LIFE

INFORMATION

SHOP

STRUCTURES

SNACK SHOP

TIME

AUDITORIUM

CITY

CULTURE

MEN

MAIN ENTRANCE

WOMEN

ACTIVITY ROOM

ADMINISTRATION

passing an afternoon in the sweatlodge.

Both outside the building and in five sunken wells within the gallery, exhibits describe features unearthed in those very places during excavations that were carried out before the construction of the Interpretive Center.

Murals positioned throughout the building show Cahokia at its height. The 30-foot mural at the gallery entrance is a view of the city center between the peaks of the Twin Mounds, the platform and conical mounds paired at the end of the Grand Plaza opposite Monks Mound. It depicts the city's landmarks and examples of daily life in and around the plaza, with people milling about the open-air market and a game of chunkey.

The Interpretive Center's gallery is a series of exhibit islands, six exploring in detail a different aspect of Cahokia's prehistory and the seventh explaining archaeological methods. Displays at the gallery's conclusion discuss the fate of the Mississippian culture at Cahokia and chart the chronology of the site in historic times.

(BELOW) Exhibit island describing structures built by the Cahokians.
(ABOVE RIGHT) The Cahokia Mounds Interpretive Center.

The Building And Exhibits Design/Construction

The 33,000 square-foot Cahokia Mounds Interpretive Center opened to the public in September 1989. It was designed and erected primarily by nearby Illinois and St. Louis-area firms at a cost of $8.2 million. The center's principal architects, engineers, and building contractors were, respectively, AAI/ Campbell, Inc. of Collinsville; Booker Associates, Inc. of Fairview Heights; and Korte Construction of Highland, all in Illinois.

The architects were challenged to create a design that was both enduring and worthy of a UNESCO World Heritage Site. They chose masonry for its timeless quality and the neutral beige facade and low profile to compliment the overall site, rather than to compete with or attempt to replicate the mounds themselves.

The low-lying site of the proposed Interpretive Center had never been thoroughly investigated by archaeologists. To prevent the loss of potentially priceless knowledge, Southern Illinois University at Edwardsville conducted excavations there prior to construction, from 1985 to 1987.

Their work revealed significant and surprising information about the prehistoric use of the area. First, it was the site of three previously unknown mounds, two of which have been reconstructed and the third protected by redesigning the parking lot.

Second, contrary to popular belief, it also had been a residential neighborhood during at least four phases of Cahokia's occupation. In addition, the excavations produced recommendations that determined the eventual shape of the building.

Several other features of the Interpretive Center are especially noteworthy. They include an expansive glass wall that gives a panoramic view across the Grand Plaza to Monks Mound; the mirror village, considered the largest magnification effect of its kind ever attempted; and the entry vestibule whose walls and massive doors are faced with bronze panels with bas-relief designs that incorporate human and bird figures, the Stockade, and a profile of Monks Mound.

Artist Preston Jackson of Peoria, Illinois designed the entryway and sculpted the doors in beeswax. The exterior doors, cast by Scott Metals of Indianapolis, Indiana, were funded entirely by the State of Illinois, whose budget for the Interpretive Center included up to a 1 percent allowance for works of art by an Illinois artist. The interior doors, cast later by Art Casting of Illinois of Oregon, Illinois, were made possible by a $60,000 gift, most of it from a single benefactor. Additional donations by the general public and the Cahokia Mounds Museum Society provided funding for the installation of the doors.

The permanent exhibits in the Cahokia Mounds Interpretive Center were planned and designed by Gerard Hilferty and Associates of Athens, Ohio, and produced by Design Craftsmen, Inc. of Midland, Michigan.

Life-size figures were created using Native American models by Sculpture Basis, Brooklyn, New York; structures and miniature dioramas by Beverly Mosely and Associates of Grove City, Ohio; and all audio-visual productions by Donna Lawrence Productions, Inc. of Louisville, Kentucky.

The Cahokia Mounds Interpretive Center has won national awards for its multimedia orientation show, masonry work, and architectural design.

(LEFT) The bronze entryway to the Cahokia Mounds Interpretive Center. Images on exterior, shown here, include birds in flight and combat and profile of Monks Mound. Interior incorporates human figures and Stockade. (BELOW) Tour group observing excavation of Grand Plaza.

Programs and Services

The Cahokia Mounds State Historic Site and Interpretive Center offer a wide variety of programs and services throughout the year to schools and the general public. These include lecture series; seasonal guided tours; educational programs for school classes; self-guided tours with booklets written in 13 languages, including Braille; Native American arts and crafts classes; nature/culture hikes; marked interpretive trails; festival days featuring displays, demonstrations, hands-on activities, and Native American food and dancing; a year-round, 10-kilometer Volksmarch trail; trips to other archaeological sites; and sunrise observances at the recon-

Native Americans at Prehistoric Lifeways, Cahokia's largest annual festival.

structed Woodhenge sun calendar, both at the winter and summer solstices and the spring and autumn equinoxes. Various institutions conduct archaeological and educational field schools at Cahokia.

In addition to its permanent displays, the Interpretive Center has a space for temporary exhibits that change regularly. The Museum Shop stocks a large selection of books as well as Native American art and jewelry, and Cafe Cahokia offers snacks.

A large volunteer organization assists in all aspects of the site's operation.

(TOP) Children cracking nuts at annual Native Harvest Festival.
(TOP RIGHT) The Museum Shop in lobby of Interpretive Center.
(ABOVE) Native American demonstrating beadwork on moccasin.
(RIGHT) Choctaw split-cane basket class.

The Cahokia Mounds State Historic Site and Interpretive Center are administered by the Illinois Historic Preservation Agency with support from the privately funded, not-for-profit Cahokia Mounds Museum Society. These organizations are committed to ongoing preservation, restoration, research, and interpretation at Cahokia and to continued expansion of the protected area.

For more information about the Cahokia Mounds State Historic Site, contact:

Cahokia Mounds State
Historic Site
30 Ramey Street
Collinsville, Illinois 62234
(618) 346-5160

www.cahokiamounds.com

CAHOKIA
MOUNDS
MUSEUM SOCIETY